DAY BY DAY WITH...

WILLOW SMITH

BY
TAMRA ORR

Mitchell Lane
PUBLISHERS
P.O. Box 196
Hockessin, Delaware 19707
Visit us on the web: www.mitchelllane.com
Comments? email us:
mitchelllane@mitchelllane.com

Mitchell Lane
PUBLISHERS

Printing   1   2   3   4   5   6   7   8   9

RANDY'S CORNER

DAY BY DAY WITH...

Beyoncé	Miley Cyrus
Dwayne "The Rock" Johnson	Selena Gomez
Eli Manning	Shaun White
Justin Bieber	Taylor Swift
LeBron James	Willow Smith

Library of Congress Cataloging-in-Publication Data
Orr, Tamra.
 Day by day with Willow Smith / by Tamra Orr.
    p. cm.
 Includes bibliographical references and index.
 ISBN 978-1-58415-983-4 (library bound)
 1. Willow, 2000– – Juvenile literature. 2. Actors – United States – Biography – Juvenile literature. 3. Singers – United States – Biography – Juvenile literature. I. Title.
 PN2287.S6123O77 2011
 792.02′8092 – dc23
 [B]
                                                                    2011036822
eBook ISBN: 9781612281513

ABOUT THE AUTHOR: Tamra Orr is a full-time author living in the Pacific Northwest with her family. She has written over 250 books for kids of all ages, including celebrity biographies for Mitchell Lane Publishers (*Shia LaBeouf, Brenda Song, Robert Pattinson,* and *Jordin Sparks*). Orr loves reading all kinds of books, plus writing letters to friends across the globe.

PLB

DAY BY DAY WITH

WILLOW SMITH

Willow Camille Reign Smith was born on Halloween in Los Angeles, California. She joined brothers Trey and Jaden.

THE UNITED STATES OF AMERICA

California

Los Angeles

JAD

TREY

WILLOW, BORN OCTOBER 31, 2000

MOM

DJ JAZZY JEFF (LEFT) WITH DAD

Willow's mother, Jada Pinkett Smith, and father, Will Smith, are both famous actors on TV and in movies. Willow's brother Jaden has been in movies too.

JADEN

WILLOW LOVES
GOING TO MOVIE
PREMIERES.

By the time she was seven, Willow had starred in a movie. It was called *I Am Legend*. Her costar was her father, Will Smith!

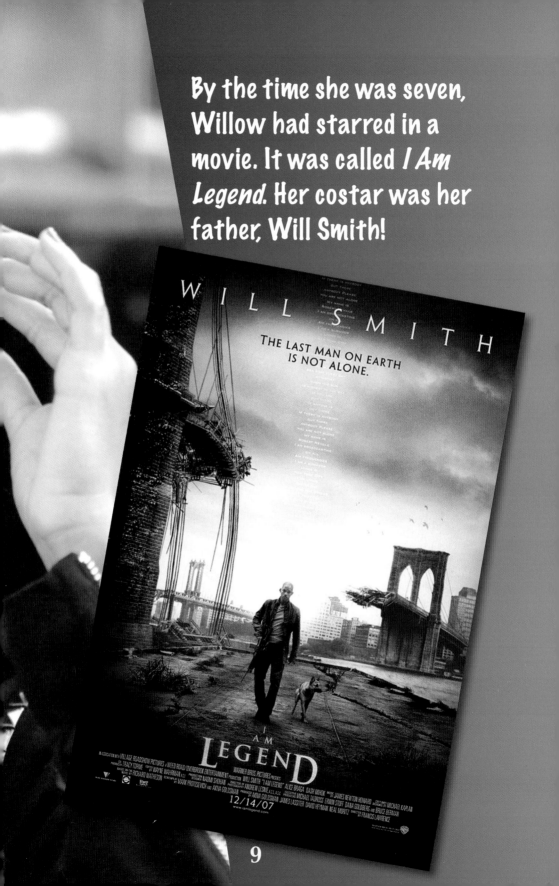

In 2008, Willow was in a movie with Abigail Breslin. It was called *Kit Kittredge: An American Girl*. For her role as Countee Garby, she won a Young Artist Award for Best Performance in a film.

ABIGAIL BRESLIN

The Hobos

ACADEMY AWARD® NOMINEE
ABIGAIL BRESLIN is
KIT
KITTREDGE
An American Girl

Her next movie role used only her voice. Willow played baby Gloria in the movie *Madagascar: Escape to Africa*. Her mother played the voice of grown-up Gloria. Willow has also played on Keke Palmer's show *True Jackson, VP*. She played young True.

GLORIA

KEKE PALMER

Willow gets interviewed a lot on TV shows such as BET's *106 & Park* with Terrence J. and Rocsi and *The Ellen Degeneres Show*. With all the time she spends working, she cannot go to regular school. Instead, her mother homeschools her.

Jaden and Willow want to help other people around the world. They became youth ambassadors for Project Zambia. It helps children in Africa with AIDS. "Project Zambia is about kids and for kids, and it's so important that we all learn to take care of each other," Jaden and Willow said.

LADY
GAGA

Like most young people, Willow loves music. "I like the way Billy Idol sings. Mommy turned me on to him. And I like Lady Gaga's songs," says Willow.

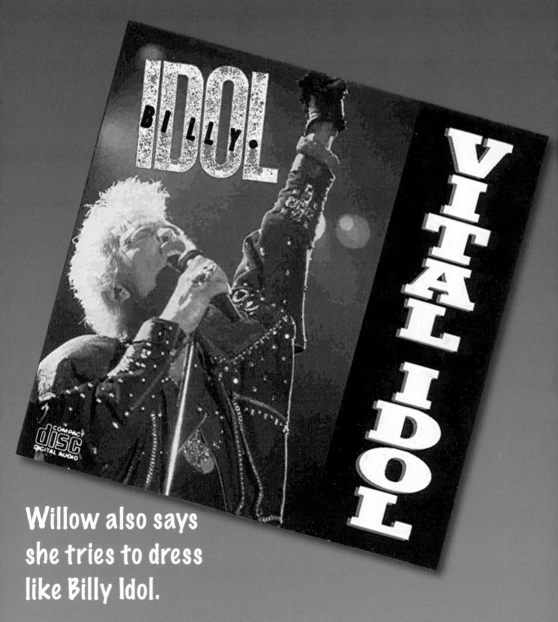

Willow also says she tries to dress like Billy Idol.

MOM

MICHELLE
OBAMA

In late 2010, Willow recorded the song "Whip My Hair." It was a huge hit! Willow says her music style is "punk rock meets preppy." The Obama daughters Malia and

MALIA
OBAMA

JADEN

Sasha like her music so much that Willow was asked to play a concert at the White House.

21

JAY-Z

JUSTIN BIEBER

It was not long after her song came out that Jay-Z's record label signed Willow to do a whole album. She went on tour with Justin Bieber in 2011. The two would perform all across Europe.

PERFORMING AT A HOLIDAY CONCERT

Her song was played on radio stations all across the country. Willow also got the chance to sing the song on *Dick Clark's New Year's Rockin' Eve with Ryan Seacrest* as well as for the L.A. LIVE concert.

ON TOUR WITH JUSTIN BIEBER

Along with acting and singing, Willow also loves clothes. She wears bright colors and wild outfits. She says, "If I had my own fashion company, I would call it Willow's Reign."

What is next for Willow? As she told one magazine, "I get my flow from daddy, my singing ability from mommy, and the camera

stuff from both. That's just what happens when you hang out with the Smiths!"

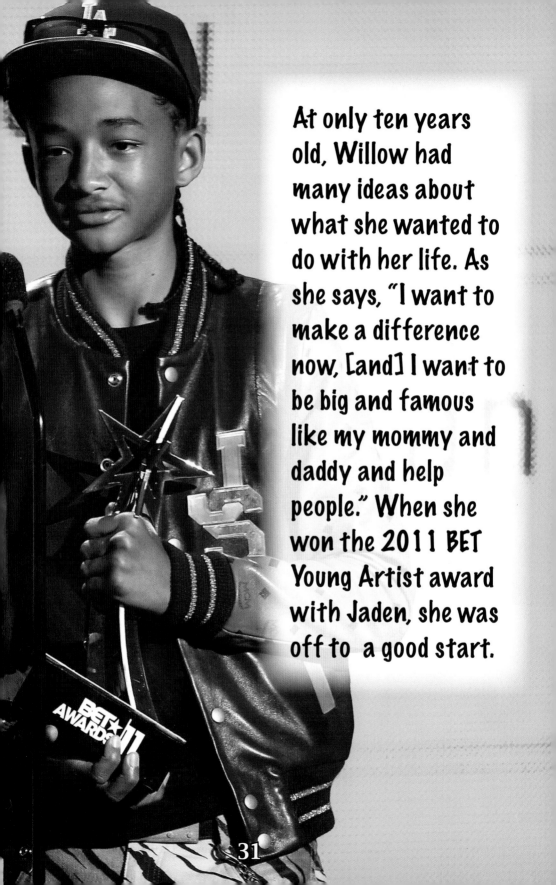

At only ten years old, Willow had many ideas about what she wanted to do with her life. As she says, "I want to make a difference now, [and] I want to be big and famous like my mommy and daddy and help people." When she won the 2011 BET Young Artist award with Jaden, she was off to a good start.

FURTHER READING

Books

If you enjoyed this book about Willow Smith, you might also enjoy the following Day By Day books from Mitchell Lane Publishers:

Beyoncé
Justin Bieber
Miley Cyrus
Selena Gomez
Taylor Swift

On the Internet

CBS News Image Gallery
http://www.cbsnews.com/2300-500150_162-2366342.html
Willow Smith
http://www.willowsmith.com;
Willow Smith Fan Site
http://www.willow-smith.org

Works Consulted

Grant, Meg. "Will Power." *Reader's Digest*. December 2006. http://www.rd.com/family/will-smith-interview/
"Jaden and Willow Smith Support Project Zambia." *In Touch Weekly*. October 7, 2009. http://www.intouchweekly.com/2009/10/jaden_and_willow_smith_support.php
Smith, Krista. *Vanity Fair*, February 2011.
"Willow Smith and Jaden Smith." *Glamour/Vanity*. http://www.glamourvanity.com/willow-jaden-smith/
Willow Smith Bio. KidzWorld. http://www.kidzworld.com/article/24878-willow-smith-bio

INDEX

PHOTO CREDITS: Cover design—Joe Rasemas; pp. 3, 7—Jemal Countess/Getty Images; p. 5—FilmMagic; p. 6—Dave Morgan/Alpha/Globe Photos; p. 8—Nancy Carradine; pp. 10–11—AP Photo/Chris Pizzello; pp. 12–13—PRNewsFoto/Nickelodeon, Peter Stone/Nickelodeon; p. 14—Johnny Nunez/WireImage; p. 18—WireImage; pp. 20–21—Getty Images; p. 21—Mandel Ngan/AFP/Getty Images; pp. 22–23—WireImage; p. 24—John Sciulli/WireImage; p. 25—Michael Tran/FilmMagic; p. 26—Chris Lopez/Getty Images; p. 27—Christopher Polk/KCA2011/Getty Images; pp. 28–29—Chris Jackson/Getty Images; pp. 30–31—Joe Scarnici/WireImage. All other photos—CreativeCommons. Every effort has been made to locate all copyright holders of materials used in this book. Any errors or omissions will be corrected in future editions of the book.